W9-CPD-188

YOUR LAND AND MY LAND

The Middle East

We Visit

PAKISTAN

Bonnie

Hinman

Mitchell Lane

PUBLISHERS
P.O. Box 196
Hockessin, Delaware 19707

YOUR LAND
AND
MY LAND
The Middle East

Afghanistan
Iran
Iraq
Israel
Kuwait
Oman
Pakistan
Saudi Arabia
Turkey
Yemen

We Visit

PAKISTAN

Mitchell Lane
PUBLISHERS

Printing   1   2   3   4   5   6   7   8   9

Library of Congress Cataloging-in-Publication Data
Hinman, Bonnie.
  We visit Pakistan / by Bonnie Hinman.
      p. cm. — (Your land and my land: the Middle East)
  Includes bibliographical references and index.
  ISBN 978-1-58415-960-5 (library bound)
  1. Pakistan—Juvenile literature. I. Title.
  DS376.9.H56 2011
  954.91—dc23
                                                                    2011030763
eBook ISBN: 9781612281032

PUBLISHER'S NOTE: This story is based on the author's extensive research, which she believes to be accurate. Documentation of this research is on page 60.

The Internet sites referenced herein were active as of the publication date. Due to the fleeting nature of some web sites, we cannot guarantee they will all be active when you are reading this book.

To reflect current usage, we have chosen to use the secular era designations BCE ("before the common era") and CE ("of the common era") instead of the traditional designations BC ("before Christ") and AD (*anno Domini,* "in the year of the Lord").

Contents

The Sindh High Court in Karachi, Pakistan

Introduction

The term *Middle East* was first used to describe the countries stretching east from Israel and Lebanon to the eastern edge of Iran. It went south to Saudi Arabia and Yemen and north to Syria. Today the name usually includes Turkey in the northwest and sometimes Egypt and parts of Africa to the southwest. Pakistan and Afghanistan on the east are sometimes also included.

The Middle East has a rich and ancient cultural history. Several of the world's first civilizations started there, including the Indus Valley Civilization in Pakistan. Many trading routes crisscrossed the mountains, valleys, and deserts of the Middle East, linking China and Europe. These trading routes are usually called the Silk Road but are actually a series of roads that link parts of China to Africa, Central Asia, India, Turkey, and the Mediterranean area of Europe. The earliest report of a traveler on the Silk Road was from 959 BCE, almost 3,000 years ago.[1]

Pakistan is home to many different ethnic groups, all of which have a history of passion for their heritage. In spite of regular political problems and conflicts, Pakistanis are generally friendly and welcoming to visitors. There are a great many different languages, and

some outsiders find it difficult to communicate in Pakistan—but any effort to learn a few words of the local language is richly rewarded. It is one clue to the generosity of the Pakistani people.

 Much of Pakistan is dry and ranges from permanent snow and cold of the high elevations to the coastal mangroves. The Indus River winds through it all from the mountain valleys of the north to the mudflats of the delta in the south.

The Mighty Indus

The backbone of Pakistan's ancient towns and cities is the Indus River, which flows from north to south. It begins in Tibet in China, high in the Himalaya, then travels northwest through the Indian Kashmir region and turns south in Gilgit-Baltistan. The 1,900-mile- (3,100-kilometer-) long river runs through mountains, deserts, and plateaus until it empties into the Arabian Sea near the Pakistani city of Karachi.

The Indus River Valley is the birthplace of one of the oldest civilizations in the world. An organized and urbanized civilization existed there as long ago as 3300 BCE. The Indus Valley Civilization had its golden period at the same time as Egypt was building the pyramids thousands of miles to the west.

Two of the Indus Valley cities discovered were Harappa and Mohenjo-Daro. Both had huge stone buildings and monuments. It was apparent to archaeologists that these cities had been planned and must have had some kind of municipal governments. Remnants of ancient sanitation systems were found in the form of covered drains, which lined the larger streets. The people were skilled engineers and traders. They were part of a trading network that stretched to Mesopotamia to the west and India to the east.

Evidence of a written language has been found, including more than 400 symbols or characters on seals, tablets, and ceramic pots. Some of this writing can be seen on seals in the National Museum of Pakistan in Karachi.

The Indus Valley Civilization began a gradual decline around 1800 BCE. The valley cooled a great deal and got drier about the same time as the cities began to disappear. Earthquakes may have changed the course of smaller rivers. Whatever the cause, people abandoned their cities.

After more than a thousand years of peace in the Indus Valley, the area was invaded over and over for several hundred years. Aryan nomadic tribes from Central Asia spilled over the area around 1500 BCE and stayed for 500 years.

King Darius I of Persia marched through in 518 BCE and demanded taxes from the people. In 327 BCE, Alexander the Great of Macedonia pushed into the region but found the locals to be fierce fighters. He was forced to float his army down the Indus River on rafts to the Arabian Sea.

The Maurans, Bactrians, Scythians, and Parthians passed through the Indus Valley, too. The Kushans brought Buddhism, while the Shahi dynasty, which took control around 870 CE, was largely responsible for the spread of Hinduism.

Meanwhile, starting in the seventh century, a new and powerful religion began far to the west of the Indus Valley. In Mecca, Saudi Arabia, an Arab merchant named Muhammad founded a new religion called Islam. It spread quickly through most of the Middle East and Persia.

Islam arrived in Pakistan around 711 CE when an Arab army invaded Sindh. The Arab leader, Muhammad bin Qasim, tried three times to subdue Sindh and finally succeeded. Many Sindh citizens converted to Islam in the aftermath of the invasions.[1]

Several Muslim empires followed, but the Mughal Empire was the last and most influential for Pakistan and India. The first Mughal emperor, Babur, was a descendant of Genghis Khan. Babur came from Turkistan in the north after his father died. He was only twelve years old, and his older relatives rejected him as the new ruler.

Babur arrived in India in 1526. He conquered most of northern India, including the area that is now Pakistan. The Mughal Empire he founded endured until 1858 when the British ousted Bahadur Shah Zafar, the last Mughal ruler.[2]

The Mughals enriched the areas they conquered in dozens of ways. Mughal emperors were tolerant of other religious beliefs and ran their governments with respect for human rights. They introduced Persian art and culture and encouraged the mixture of the Persian language with Arabic and Hindi, creating Urdu, modern Pakistan's official language.

The visible proof of the Mughal Empire is in the architecture it left behind. Besides the Taj Mahal in India, the Mughals also built the Lahore Fort and other buildings in Lahore, Pakistan, which was the capital of their empire.

The British ruled India from the mid-1800s until independence and partition in 1947. Their empire was called the British Raj. They used Lahore and Rawalpindi as regional district centers. There they built cantonments—separate areas where the British officials and their families lived.

During the fiercely hot Punjabi summers, the British fled to what they called the hill towns or stations. Whole segments of the government sometimes moseyed to the hills. Many of these resort towns or villages, such as Murree, continue to serve as resorts.

When India became independent in 1947, India and Pakistan were partitioned, or separated into two countries. It was a grand day when Pakistan was declared free, but there would be problems for the country carved out of an ancient kingdom.

Construction of Lahore Museum began in 1890 as a tribute to Queen Victoria's Golden Jubilee.

It houses paintings that date back to Mughal, Sikh, and British times.

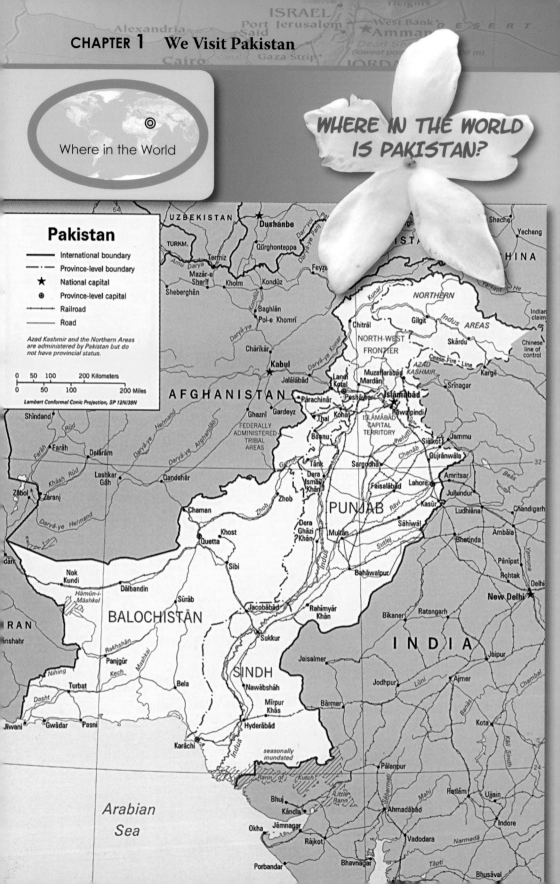

Where in the World

WHERE IN THE WORLD
IS PAKISTAN?

Pakistan

—————— International boundary
—·—·—·— Province-level boundary
★ National capital
◉ Province-level capital
⊢⊣⊢⊣⊢⊣ Railroad
—————— Road

Azad Kashmir and the Northern Areas
are administered by Pakistan but do
not have provincial status.

0   50   100   200 Kilometers
0   50   100   200 Miles

Lambert Conformal Conic Projection, SP 12N/38N

PAKISTAN FACTS AT A GLANCE

Full name: Islamic Republic of Pakistan

Official languages: Urdu and English

Population: 187,342,721 (July 2011 est.)

Land area: 307,374 square miles (796,095 square kilometers); roughly twice the size of California

Capital: Islamabad

Government: Federal Republic

Ethnic makeup: Punjabi, Pashtun, Sindhi, Sariaki, Muhajirs, and Balochi

Religions: Islam 95% (Sunni 75%, Shia 20%), other (includes Christianity and Hinduism) 5%

Exports: Textiles, rice, leather goods, sports goods, chemicals, manufactures, carpets and rugs

Imports: Petroleum, petroleum products, machinery, plastics, transportation equipment, edible oils, paper and paperboard, iron and steel, tea

Crops: Cotton, wheat, rice, sugarcane, fruits, vegetables

Average temperatures: August 88°F (31°C); January 55°F (13°C)

Average rainfall: 19.3 inches (490 millimeters)

Highest point: K2 (Mt. Godwin-Austin)—28,251 feet (8,611 meters)

Longest river: Indus—1,976 miles (3,180 kilometers)

Flag: Pakistan's flag is green with a vertical white band, which symbolizes the role of religious minorities, on the hoist side. A large white crescent and star are centered in the green field. The crescent, star, and color green are traditional symbols of Islam.

National flower: Jasmine (*Jasminum*)

National bird: Chakor, or red-legged partridge (*Alectoris chukar*)

National tree: Deodar cedar (*Cedrus deodara*)

Sources: CIA *World Factbook:* "Pakistan"; Pakistan Climate Guide (http://www.climatetemp.info/pakistan/)

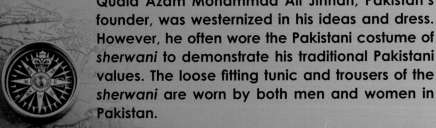

Quaid Azam Mohammad Ali Jinnah, Pakistan's founder, was westernized in his ideas and dress. However, he often wore the Pakistani costume of *sherwani* to demonstrate his traditional Pakistani values. The loose fitting tunic and trousers of the *sherwani* are worn by both men and women in Pakistan.

Pakistan: A Young Country

The years after partition have not been easy or peaceful for Pakistanis. There has been fighting among the different ethnic and tribal groups, and between conservative Islamic groups and more moderate ones. Tribal, ethnic, and religious differences have kept the Pakistanis from working together.

Pakistan's government is called a federal parliamentary system. The constitution that was approved in 1973 names Islam as the state religion, and states that the president must be Muslim. The president is elected for a five-year term and can serve no more than two terms in a row. He or she is chosen by an electoral college consisting of members of the two legislative bodies, the Senate and the National Assembly.

The prime minister, who is in charge of the day-to-day operations of the government, is appointed by the president, who chooses from members of the National Assembly. The president usually acts on the advice of the prime minister but has one unique power. He can dissolve the National Assembly if he feels an issue needs to be taken back to the voters.

Voters in each district elect the National Assembly, or lower house members. The number of representatives depends on the population. Each of the four provinces, plus the Federally Administered Tribal Areas, the Islamabad Capital Territory, and the state of Gilgit-Baltistan, elect members to the National Assembly.

Individual provincial assemblies or similar bodies elect the Senate, or upper house members. The chairman of the Senate is next in line to the presidency, should the office become vacant during the president's term.

Pakistan has a Supreme Court and other lower courts for civil and criminal cases. Supreme Court judges are appointed by the president and serve until age sixty-five. There is also a Federal Sharia Court, which has eight Muslim judges, three of whom are experts in Islamic law. This court decides whether a law agrees with the rules of Islam.

The military has always had a strong influence on Pakistani politics and still does. By 2011, Pakistan had had sixteen leaders (presidents, governors general, or administrators) since Pakistan was founded in 1947. Four of them are described as chief martial law administrators, meaning that the military was in charge of the country.[1]

Muhammad Ali Jinnah was the first leader of the newborn country. He was appointed the governor general of Pakistan on August 15, 1947, a day after independence was declared.

Jinnah was born in Karachi on December 25, 1876. His parents had moved to Sindh from Kathiawar, Gujarat, before his birth. His father was a successful merchant in Karachi.

Jinnah traveled to London in 1892 to start an apprenticeship at a shipping company. However, he soon left there and studied law at Lincoln's Inn in London.

Jinnah lived in England for several years before returning to his homeland. In 1896 he joined the Indian National Congress. Later he also joined the All India Muslim League and took on leadership roles in both organizations. These organizations worked toward making India independent of Pakistan.

At first Jinnah favored a united India, with Muslims and Hindus (the major religious group of the British-occupied territory) cooperating in government and society. Eventually he decided that the Muslims must have a separate country. He believed it would be impossible for them to achieve fair treatment in a country dominated by Hindus.

After much negotiation, all parties agreed to partition—to separate sections of British India from the rest of it. West Pakistan was separated from East Pakistan by Nepal and part of India.

After he became governor general of the new Pakistan, Jinnah worked tirelessly to set up all the institutions a new country needs. However, he was seriously ill during this time and died on September 11, 1948.

Although Pakistan was founded as a Muslim nation, Jinnah intended that all citizens freely practice their religions. It was not until the 1980s that it became illegal to practice other religions or speak anything against Islam. This Islamization of Pakistan was in direct opposition to Jinnah's intent.

Jinnah is greatly revered by Pakistanis. He is often called Quaid-e Azam (Great Leader) and Baba-e-Qaum (Father of the Nation). His birthday, December 25, is celebrated as a national holiday throughout Pakistan.

Historian Stanley Wolpert wrote of Jinnah, "Few individuals significantly alter the course of history. Fewer still modify the map of the world. Hardly anyone can be credited with creating a nation-state. [Muhammad] Ali Jinnah did all three."[2]

**Chief Justice
Agha Rafiq Ahmed Khan**

Munir Ahmad Khan (right) headed the Pakistan Atomic Energy Commission when President Zulfikar Ali Bhutto asked him to do a survey of progress made toward Pakistan's becoming a nuclear power. Munir Ahmad Khan was later overshadowed by A.Q. Khan, who claimed to be the true father of the nuclear program in Pakistan.

Generals, Presidents, and Prime Ministers

Many Pakistanis believe that if Jinnah had lived longer, Pakistan might have traveled a different path. The three civilian governors general that came after Jinnah were not up to the job. Two of them abused their power to the point that by the mid 1950s, only the army could maintain control in the streets. The military staged a coup in 1958.[1]

General Ayub Khan ruled Pakistan for eleven years. He made some economic improvements and presided over the capital's move from Karachi to the new city of Islamabad. General Yahya Khan overthrew him in 1969.

This khan held the first national elections in East and West Pakistan in 1970. The vote confirmed that East Pakistanis wanted more freedom to govern themselves.

Ayub Khan responded by sending tanks to subdue the troublemakers. East Pakistanis retaliated, and India supported them in the war. The West Pakistani army was defeated, and the new nation of Bangladesh was born of East Pakistan in 1971.[2]

Zulfikar Ali Bhutto took over from Ayub Khan the same year as martial law administrator. Bhutto was born in 1928 into a prominent Sindhi Muslim family. He was educated in India, the United States, and Great Britain, and became the youngest member of Pakistan's United Nations delegation in 1957.

Bhutto had held several ministry positions under President Ayub Khan. He was appointed foreign minister for Pakistan in 1962. He resigned his post in 1966 because of a disagreement with President Ayub Khan.

Bhutto started a new political party in 1966. The Pakistan People's Party (PPP) inspired many Pakistanis with its socialist and Islamic ideals. When Ayub Khan was forced out, Bhutto was in the right place to take over management of martial law.

In 1972 when Bhutto was Minister for Fuel, Power and Natural Resources, he initiated Pakistan's nuclear program. The arrival of Dr. Abdul Qadeer "A.Q." Khan in 1975 to take over the development of Pakistan's nuclear development program was a huge step forward. Dr. Khan was a German-educated metallurgist who directed a secret program to develop nuclear weapons. By 1985 Pakistan could produce weapons-grade uranium, and a little more than a decade later—in 1998—conducted nuclear tests.

In 1973 Bhutto was elected prime minister and continued his campaign to increase his control over every aspect of Pakistan's government and economy. There was more nationalization of industries and harsh repression of any critics.[3]

In 1977 Bhutto was reelected as prime minister, but there was widespread rigging of the election. Antigovernment protesters were shot and killed at demonstrations in favor of a new election. The army stepped in and martial law was once more declared, with General Muhammad Zia-ul-Haq in charge.

General Zia had Bhutto arrested. On April 4, 1979, Zia had the former leader executed.[4] Zia was known as a hard-core Islamist. He went on an 11-year-campaign to make the government, economy, and Pakistani society in general conform strictly to Sharia (Islamic law).[5]

General Zia was killed in a plane crash in August 1988. The cause of the crash was never determined but reports issued after an investigation suggested that the plane was sabotaged.

With Banazir Bhutto as prime minister, democracy returned to Pakistan for eleven years. For most of that time the powerful Bhutto and the Sharif families traded power back and forth.

Benazir Bhutto was the daughter of Zulfikar Ali Bhutto and heir to a large estate in Sindh. Her roots were in the traditional feudal system. Her major rival for power, Nawaz Sharif belonged to a powerful self-made industrial family. Benazir Bhutto's father nationalized the Sharif family's foundry in 1972. There has been bad blood between the two families ever since.

Democratic accomplishments were few during the years controlled by either Bhutto or Sharif. Bhutto was educated in the West and was generally more tolerant of criticism aimed at her by the media. She was interested in being modern in her approach to government. Sharif was not Western-educated and was far more sympathetic to Islamic issues. He was not a modernist and often cracked down on non-Muslim government groups. Both were willing to do whatever it took to stay in power.

A military coup in 1999 replaced Sharif with General Pervez Musharraf. Musharraf became chief executive of Pakistan and a later referendum made him president. He made a promise when he took over: "I shall not allow the people to be taken back to the era of sham democracy, but to a true one."[6]

General Muhammad Zia-ul-Haq seized control of Pakistan in a coup in July 1977. He set out to Islamicize Pakistan. He introduced punishments such as two-month prison sentences for eating or drinking during daylight hours of Ramadan, cutting off a thief's hand, and public whippings for many other offenses.

Benazir Bhutto and Asif Ali Zardari at their wedding in 1987. Bhutto's father, Zulfikar Ali Bhutto, was executed in April 1979. For most of the next six years, Benazir Bhutto was under house arrest or imprisoned. She was allowed to leave the country in 1984 for medical reasons. She returned to Pakistan in 1986.

The people considered Musharraf a big improvement over their recent leaders. He was able to obtain a great deal of foreign aid from the United States, which helped the Pakistani economy to rebound from bankruptcy. His economic policies also helped Pakistan's bottom line improve.

Both Benazir Bhutto and her husband Asif Ali Zardari were charged with corruption, as was Nawaz Sharif. All three went into exile either to delay prosecution or as part of a deal made with the Musharraf government.

Musharraf was unable to turn Pakistan toward the democracy he had promised. He was unable or unwilling to seriously tackle some of the toughest issues, like taxation. Very few Pakistanis paid any kind of taxes, and this didn't really change.

The September 11, 2001, terrorist attacks on the United States put Pakistan in the news. Afghanistan was the original target of the War on Terror, as the effort to suppress terror groups was called. Afghanistan provided assistance to the al-Qaeda groups, including hiding places and money. At the time of 9/11, the Taliban was in control of Afghanistan. The Taliban government was an extremist Islamic one, but it was not a part of al-Qaeda.

Pakistan also harbored al-Qaeda groups particularly in the regions that bordered Afghanistan. Officially Pakistan supported the effort to oust the Taliban and al-Qaeda, but it was well known that both groups moved freely about the country. U.S. demands that Pakistan actively pursue the terrorists contrasted with obligations to fellow Muslims. These opposite goals kept Pakistan in the hot seat over the Taliban and al-Qaeda. By 2007, Pakistan was seething with unrest.

In October of that year, Benazir Bhutto, now leader of the PPP, returned triumphantly from exile but was assassinated two months later, on December 27. Her husband, Asif Ali Zardari, took over leadership of the PPP.

Unrest continued until Musharraf resigned. Elections were held, and Zardari was elected president. He took office in September 2008. His path has not been easy. Old problems have not been resolved, and new ones crop up frequently.

Zardari was criticized for the government's slow response during and after the floods of July and August 2010. He still faced corruption charges. The United States pressured Pakistan to do its part to get rid of al-Qaeda fighters who roamed between Pakistan and Afghanistan. The U.S. also believed that al-Qaeda leader Osama bin Laden was hidden somewhere in the mountainous tribal areas in western Pakistan. As it turned out, Bin Laden was hiding in Pakistan but not in the tribal areas. He was in the town of Abbottabad less than 60 miles (100 kilometers) from Islamabad. This discovery and the covert U.S. operation to kill Bin Laden in May 2011 strained relations between Pakistan and the United States.

Modern Pakistan is not an easy place to visit, but each province offers wonders of nature, art, and history.

Karachi's Clifton Beach isn't suitable for swimming but is a popular destination to take a stroll. Camel and horse rides are also available, along with cold drinks and grilled corn.

Sindh Province

Sindh Province takes its name from the Indus River, which flows through the province's midsection. In ancient times the Indus was called the Sindhus. Sindh is in the southeast corner of Pakistan, bordered by India on the east and the Pakistan province of Balochistan on the west. Punjab Province is north of Sindh, and the Arabian Sea lies south.

On the coast of the Arabian Sea lies the city of Karachi, Pakistan's only major ocean port. This huge sprawling city has over 18 million people and is growing by more than 4 percent a year. It was the capital of Pakistan from the country's founding in 1947 until 1959, and now it is the capital of Sindh Province.

Karachi is an exciting cosmopolitan city populated with people of many different cultures and ethnic backgrounds. Its strong economic base as the Pakistani center of banking, industry, and trade has lured migrants from other provinces in Pakistan. After partition, Muslims from India fled to Karachi. The Indian Muslims, called Mohajirs, became a major force in local leadership and economic success.[1]

Pashtuns, Punjabis, and descendants of the Mohajirs have long competed with the local Sindhis for economic and political power. This has given Karachi a reputation for unrest and conflict among its residents. The city has also become home to an ever-increasing tide of refugees from Afghanistan.

Karachi is considered a dangerous place to visit. It has been known as a base for al-Qaeda and some of the Afghan Taliban. Rumors persisted for years that Bin Laden was hiding in Karachi. He was known to have gone to Karachi for treatment of a shrapnel injury in 2002, and many believed he had gone back.

Karachi has many reminders of British colonial days. The Empress Market, for example, is a huge indoor market area named after Queen Victoria, known as the Empress of India when it opened in 1889. The market's tall clock tower dominates the skyline in the Saddar area of Karachi. Inside the covered bazaar is a maze of merchants with their wares and storefronts offering services. Many are roadside dentists. Salesmen crowd the narrow sidewalks to tempt people inside for dental work.

Karachi is a small part of Sindh Province, which is rural and subtropical, with hot summers and cold winters. Sindh is arid, averaging only 6–7 inches (15–18 centimeters) of rain a year. The Great Thar Desert occupies the southwestern part of Sindh that borders India.

In spite of so little rain, Sindh successfully grows many crops. Extensive irrigation includes damming the Indus at Sukkur. The water is diverted into canals that snake through the delta to water the crops. The fertile delta plain around the Indus River grows wheat, rice, millet, cotton, sugarcane, fruits, and many other products.

The Dancing Girl of Mohenjo-Daro

The Indus also floods with snowmelt in the spring and during the monsoon season in August and September. Floods in August 2010 were particularly destructive as they drove millions of people from their homes along the Indus and its tributaries.

Southwest of Sukkur near the Indus is the ancient site of Mohenjo-Daro, built around 2600 BCE. At 1,112 acres (450 hectares), it is the largest of over 150 Indus Valley Civilization sites discovered so far. It may have been the largest urban area in the world at its peak around 2000 BCE. Archaeologists estimate that it may have had as many as 35,000 to 50,000 residents.

The streets of the ancient city are wide and carefully planned in grid patterns. Many of

Ruins of the ancient city of Mohenjo-Daro include what was called the great bath and a wealthy residential area. The great bath was lined with fired brick and sealed with watertight materials. It had a brick-lined drain. The homes of wealthy residents included pipes leading to outdoor drains.

the houses are two stories and solidly built of dried brick. Public garbage collection areas, indoor toilets, and covered drains all point toward an advanced people.

The Mohenjo-Daro Museum contains artifacts discovered at the site, including engraved seals, terracotta toys, kitchen utensils, weapons, jewelry, and other ornaments.[2]

If you travel northeast from Mohenjo-Daro and catch the National Highway, you will arrive in Punjab Province, which is home to more than half of Pakistan's population.

FYI FACT:

Between September and November, Olive Ridley and green turtles roam the coast off Karachi. These sea turtles spend most of their lives in the water.

The Mughal Lahore Fort is a fortified palace complex. Many of the buildings were constructed after the Mughals built the first structure. The fort is big enough to allow several elephants carrying dignitaries to enter at the same time. One of the stone staircases was built especially for ceremonial elephant processions.

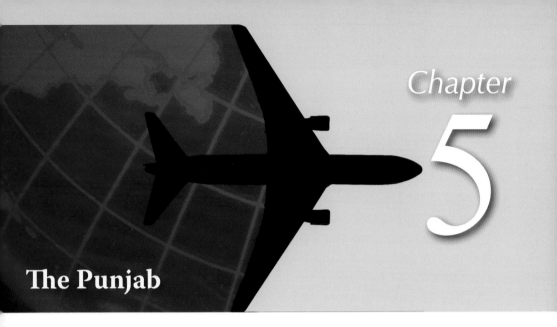

The Punjab

Punjab, whose name means "five rivers," is the second largest province in Pakistan. The Sutlej, Ravi, Beas, Jhelum, and Chenab Rivers flow to the south before they join together and flow into the Indus near the Sindh Province border.

Punjab has been in the path of conquerors since the days of the Indus Civilization. Punjabis suffered through centuries of bitter fighting and bloodshed as it was conquered by the Persians, Greeks, Kushans, Scythians, Turks, Afghans, and others.

It has also long been a center for learning and religious thought. Before the arrival of Islam, Hinduism was the main religion, but there were also Buddhists, Zoroastrians, Pagans, and Shamans. Islam is now the dominant religion in Punjab, as in all of Pakistan, but many Hindu and other cultural influences remain.

The fertile valleys that lie between the five rivers are irrigated to produce wheat, cotton, rice, corn, vegetables and many other products. Irrigation is necessary as the climate is arid. Winters are cool with some rain, and summers are quite hot, with the temperature sometimes rising as high as 110°F (43°C). The higher hill country in the north stays cooler.

Punjab is also the most industrialized province in Pakistan. Heavy machinery, electrical appliances, cement, surgical instruments, sporting goods, and many other goods are manufactured there.

If a traveler comes into Punjab via the National Highway, he will arrive at Uch Sharif, which translates to "high holy place." This small town is home to impressive Sufi shrines, which are open to everyone. Sufism is known as "Islamic Mysticism." Sufis seek direct contact with God in this life rather than in the next.

Harappa is also on this road. It is the second largest excavated Indus Valley Civilization site after Mohenjo-Daro. It has a citadel mound, granary, cemetery, and drainage system. However, Harappa's ruins have been looted over many years for the bricks. Locals use them to build houses, and the British used them when they were building the nearby railroad during their occupation.[1]

The city of Lahore could be called the jewel in Pakistan's crown. In spite of political woes and economic troubles for the rest of Pakistan, Lahore has managed to maintain prosperity and relative stability. This city of over 10 million people is considered to be the center of education, cultural, and artistic expression in Pakistan. The influence of foreign invaders can be seen in the Lahore Fort, which stands on the edge of the Old City. This tangle of narrow streets and alleyways is surrounded by walls, which have 13 gates. The fort is a sprawling complex of mosques, palaces, halls, and gardens. It was there before the Mughals arrived in the early 1500s but took on its current form in 1566 when Mughal Emperor Akbar made Lahore his capital.

Two events not to be missed in Lahore happen on Thursdays. The first showcases the best of some distinctly Muslim music—the qawwali, or Islamic devotional singing. The qawwali groups sing Sufi poetry accompanied by harmonium, tabla (twin drums), and clapping. Groups gather every Thursday afternoon at the Shrine of Data Ganj Bakhsh Hajveri to perform. The best are saved for the last hour. It is an honor to perform in this event.

Another Thursday event takes place at the Shrine of Baba Shah Jamal. Informally called Sufi Night, it features Islamic mystics or Sufis spinning, whirling, and shaking their heads in rhythm with drumbeats. The Sufis attempt to put themselves in the presence of God with their frantic intense movements. The famous Sain brothers, Gonga and Mithu, are two such Sufis. They can whirl and play the drums at breakneck speed and are much admired in Pakistan.

Pakistan's national poet, Allama Muhammad Iqbal, lived in Lahore for many years during the early twentieth century. Also a philosopher and politician, he is most famous for writing poetry that celebrates the glories of Islam, and for writing the patriotic song "Tarana-e-Hind." He is buried in Lahore, and his birthday—November 9—is celebrated as a national holiday.

One more sight to see in Punjab Province is the evening closing of the border gate between Pakistan and India at Wagah near Lahore. The Pakistani and Indian soldiers participate in a carefully planned goose-stepping, snorting, and stomping ceremony. Soldiers from both sides glare at each other, while commanding officers step forward to shake hands and salute before the flags are lowered at the same time. Grandstands hold the patriotic crowds who come to enthusiastically cheer on their country's soldiers.

After seeing Punjab Province, it's time to travel up the Grand Trunk Road to the capital of Pakistan, Islamabad, and its ancient partner, Rawalpindi.

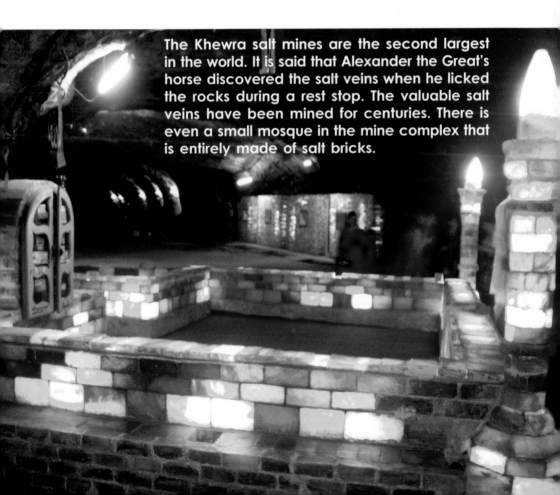

The Khewra salt mines are the second largest in the world. It is said that Alexander the Great's horse discovered the salt veins when he licked the rocks during a rest stop. The valuable salt veins have been mined for centuries. There is even a small mosque in the mine complex that is entirely made of salt bricks.

Pakistan defeated Afghanistan in an important cricket match in May 2011. Afghanistan was the first foreign cricket team to tour Pakistan since the Sri Lanka team was attacked in March 2009. Masked gunmen armed with rocket launchers attacked the Sri Lanka cricket team convoy as it traveled to a match in Lahore. Team members and coaches were injured, while six policemen and one civilian were killed in the gun battle.

Islamabad and Rawalpindi

The Pakistan capital city Islamabad and neighboring city Rawalpindi are only a few miles apart and are growing closer year by year as they both expand. Often spoken of as one big metropolitan area, the two vastly different cities depend on each other in many ways. However, Islamabad and some of the surrounding rural areas are governed separately as the Islamabad Capital Territory.

Rawalpindi, or Pindi, as locals call it, sits on the Grand Trunk Road. At least 400 years old, the Grand Trunk Road was an important trade route as well as a pathway for invaders. It extends from Calcutta, India, to Peshawar, Pakistan—over 1,600 miles (2,500 kilometers) apart.

Rawalpindi sits on a plateau that has been inhabited for thousands of years. Its fortunes rose and fell with the invaders who repeatedly captured the city. The Sikhs were the final rulers before the British occupied the city in 1849.

The British established Pindi as their military headquarters for the region. The Pakistani Armed Forces headquarters is there now. The Pakistan Army Museum displays memorabilia from colonial and modern armies. It also has a collection of ancient weapons, such as Stone Age hand axes.

Summers in Rawalpindi and elsewhere on the surrounding plateau are long and very hot. There is a monsoon season in late summer that contributes a large amount of the average 39 inches (1 meter) of rain that the area receives. The winters are mild.

The Rajah Bazaar is a good example of everyday life in an old and vibrant Pakistani city. The streets are narrow and crowded with shops and stalls selling hundreds of items. It's a good place to sample a spicy shish kebab, a popular Pakistani dish.

The game of cricket is popular in Rawalpindi. The Rawalpindi Cricket Stadium can hold more than 40,000 spectators and has a grass pitch with floodlights. International matches and exhibitions are often held there.

Pakistan has had many internationally known cricket players, including Imran Khan. Khan played for the Pakistani cricket team from 1971 to 1992. As team captain, he led the national team to victory in the 1992 World Cup. Soon after that he went into politics and was elected to the National Assembly.

In March 2011 India defeated Pakistan in the World Cup of cricket. The defeat came in the semifinal match in New Delhi. The prime ministers of the rival nations sat together in the grandstands to watch the match, hoping to point to improved relations between the neighbors. India went on to win the Cup against Sri Lanka in the finals.

Where Pindi is a sprawling old city with narrow streets that teem with traffic and people, Islamabad is a new and carefully planned capital. It is organized into sectors and zones. Designed to grow slowly outward, it has no central or downtown area.

One of the most spectacular sights in Islamabad is the Shah Faisal Mosque. Completed in 1986, it is named after King Faisal of Saudi Arabia, who gave most of the money to build it. Unlike traditional mosques with domes and arches, the Shah Faisal Mosque looks like a desert Bedouin tent.

Islamabad sits on the northern edge of the Pothohar Plateau at the foot of the Margalla Hills. Most of the year the weather in the Margallas is hot and dry. Stunted trees dot the southern slopes, while oaks and evergreens thrive on the northern side. More than 70 kinds of birds live in the Margalla Hills, including Khalij pheasants, Paradise flycatchers, Laggar falcons, and Egyptian vultures.[1]

Hikers tramping through the brush along the rocky paths need to look down as well as up at the birds. Margalla Hills has many snakes, a few of which are poisonous. Snakes to avoid are Russell's vipers,

Indian cobras, and kraits, which local Pakistanis call the half-minute killers.

Jackals can be heard cackling at night there, and wild boars are numerous. Sometimes the boars roam out of the hills into the suburbs of Islamabad. The endangered Margalla leopard lives there, as well as snow leopards and Rhesus monkeys.

Northeast of Islamabad is the former British hill station of Murree. Hill stations were established in the 1850s as summer escapes for both military and civilian families. The extreme heat and risk of cholera in Rawalpindi and other Punjab cities led the British officials to travel each summer to the Himalayan foothills. Murree and other hill stations look much like British villages, with British-style houses, churches, and shops.

One last stop northeast of Islamabad is the ancient city of Taxila. At least one excavation site there dates to the fifth century BCE. Alexander the Great made a stop in Taxila when he invaded the area in 330 BCE. The first university in Pakistan was located there, and it is a holy place to both Hindus and Buddhists. The Taxila Museum has collections of Buddha sculptures, silver and bronze artifacts, and old coins.

To the east of Islamabad and Rawalpindi lies the beautiful and troubled state of Azad Jammu & Kashmir. It is at the heart of the longest-lasting territorial dispute in the world.

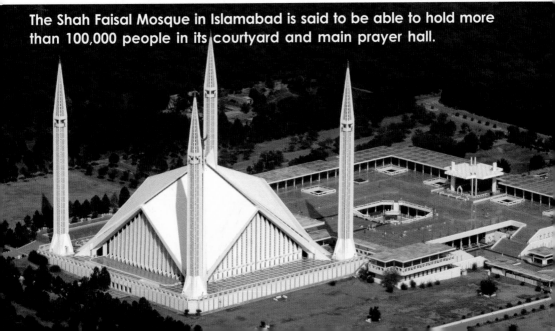

The Shah Faisal Mosque in Islamabad is said to be able to hold more than 100,000 people in its courtyard and main prayer hall.

Over 750,000 people live in Muzaffarabad, capital city of Azad Jammu & Kashmir. The city has a highly educated and business-oriented population. Muzaffarabad offers higher education opportunities for the youth all over Azad Jammu & Kashmir. The setting among mountains and along two rivers was unfortunate enough to be the epicenter of a devastating earthquake in 2005.

Chapter 7

Azad Jammu & Kashmir

Azad means "free," but while Azad Jammu & Kashmir may be called free, the state has had a heavy burden to carry since 1947 when partition occurred. Pakistan has fought wars and participated in many skirmishes against India, which also claims ownership of the area.

The princely kingdoms of India had been granted much freedom during the time of the British occupation. The maharajahs had been allowed to govern their kingdoms under British authority. When partition was agreed upon, the kingdoms were supposed to decide whether they wanted to join Pakistan or India. India was mostly Hindu, and Pakistan would be mostly Muslim.

The maharajah of Kashmir in the northwest area bordering the new nation of Pakistan had a problem. Unlike other princely kingdom leaders, he was Hindu while most of his people were Muslim. When he hesitated about joining Pakistan, the people began to revolt. Afraid of tribal warfare, the maharajah accepted help from India and linked his state with India rather than Pakistan.

This choice led almost immediately to war between India and Pakistan. There was a ceasefire in 1948, and the Line of Control was put in place. Pakistan was assigned the western edge of Kashmir while India had the rest of it.

Neither nation was happy with the division and continued to claim all of the disputed territory. Border skirmishes combined with all-out wars between India and Pakistan have continued almost without a pause since 1947. In 1989 there was a Kashmiri uprising in the India-controlled part. As many as 20,000 people were killed during the intial fighting.

In spite of the political uncertainty and violence, Azad Jammu & Kashmir has managed to give its people some advantages. Education has been a top priority, and the literacy rate there is around 65 percent, which puts it considerably higher than the Pakistani national average of 49.9 percent.

However, medical care is inadequate and the unemployment rate ranges from 30 to 50 percent. Almost 85 percent of residents live in rural areas, working in forestry, livestock, and other agricultural jobs.

Many parts of Azad Jammu & Kashmir are forested, with rivers running through the valleys that divide mountains and hills. The climate is subtropical highland. The higher the altitude, the cooler the overall climate is.

The capital city, Muzaffarabad, is located at the place where the Jhelum and the Neelum rivers meet, about 86 miles (140 kilometers) from Rawalpindi. The best-known historical site there is the Red Fort, which was built by the town's founder in 1646. Muzaffar Khan, a chief of the Chak tribe, built the fort to protect against Mughal invaders. It was rebuilt and enlarged in the 1940s. It is open to the public and has a small museum.

Muzaffarabad has a bazaar shopping area where Kashmiri crafts are sold. Brightly colored woolen shawls and walnut woodcarvings are two types of items for sale there.

On October 8, 2005, Muzaffarabad was hit by a 7.6-magnitude earthquake. The epicenter of the earthquake was a little more than 12 miles (20 kilometers) northwest of the capital city. The damaged area covered over 11,500 square miles (30,000 square kilometers). More than 80,000 people were killed in the stricken area. At least 200,000 were injured and more than 4 million people were left homeless.[1]

The northern part of Azad Jammu & Kashmir is home to many breathtaking valleys. Some travelers say that the Neelam River Valley is the most beautiful place in the world, with forested hills, snow-covered mountains, and bright blue lakes and streams. There, people can hike, fish, or take pictures.

Neelam has several villages where travelers may stay at tourist rest houses or youth hostels. These include Kundal Shahi, Dowarian, Sharda, and Kel. Near Sharda there are ruins of a Buddhist monastery or school.

In the Ganga Mountains in the far northwest part of Azad Jammu & Kashmir live brown bears, ibex, Himalayan griffon vultures, western tragopan birds, and lammergeiers, which are bearded vultures. Locals claim that the rare snow leopard lives there, too, but proof is hard to find.

Farther south are the districts of Bagh, Poonch, Kotli, and Mirpur. They are also beautiful but not on the same scale as northern Azad Jammu & Kashmir. They have small hill resorts with rest houses and a few hotels.

Many of Azad Jammu & Kashmir's river valleys were also devastated by the unusually violent monsoon rains in July and August of 2010. The Indus River and its tributaries flooded to previously unknown heights. The floodwater slowly rolled south, destroying homes, schools, businesses, and hospitals on its way to the Arabian Sea.

On a visit to Pakistan, U.N. Secretary-General Ban Ki-moon said that he had never seen anything like the devastation from the flooding there. The Secretary-General toured some of the flooded areas with Pakistan President Asif Ali Zardari. Ban said, "Thousands of towns and villages have simply been washed away. Roads, buildings, bridges, crops—millions of livelihoods have been lost. People are marooned on tiny islands with the flood waters all around them."[2]

Months later rebuilding had still barely begun. One flood survivor whose family home was destroyed was Delkhushad Shan, a kite maker. When asked how he and others would survive, Shan said, "We are at the mercy of God."[3]

North of Azad Jammu & Kashmir is Gilgit-Baltistan, home to some of the highest mountains in the world.

A landslide in January 2010 near Attabad village in the Hunza Valley blocked the Karakoram Highway (KKH) in northern Pakistan. The landslide also created a lake, which has further complicated clearing the KKH. Until the KKH is cleared, the best way to go from China to Pakistan is by boat across the newly created Lake Attabad.

Gilgit-Baltistan

Gilgit-Baltistan was called the Federally Administered Northern Areas (FANA) until September 7, 2009. The Northern Areas had been under direct control of the central Pakistani government since 1948. FANA was part of the original disputed territory of Azad Jammu & Kashmir. The new order gave autonomy to the area, and the name was changed to Gilgit-Baltistan.

Gilgit-Baltistan now has the powers and privileges of a Pakistani province, although it is not called a province. The Pakistani constitution allows for four provinces, the Islamabad Capital Territory, Federally Administered Tribal Areas, and other states and territories as may be added. Gilgit-Baltistan and Azad Jammu & Kashmir fall into the last category.

Gilgit-Baltistan has been a pathway to and from India, China, and Central Asia since ancient days. One of the Silk Road routes ran through this area to the Arabian Sea. The modern Karakoram Highway (KKH) runs through Gilgit-Baltistan along what is thought to be one of these ancient routes. The KKH starts in Islamabad and runs north to Khunjerab Pass, where the road goes into Western China. The KKH was a joint project between Pakistan and China that began in 1966. The Pakistan part of the KKH wasn't fully open until 1986. This highway runs through a countryside that had only seen donkey and camel caravans until the KKH opened.

Gilgit-Baltistan is a land of spectacular natural beauty. Three mountain ranges—Hindu Kush, Karakoram, and Himalaya—meet in this state. They contain five of the fourteen highest independent mountain peaks in the world.

At 28,251 feet (8,611 meters), K2 is the second highest mountain peak in the world. The only one higher is Mount Everest in Nepal. The other four of the five tallest are Nanga Parbat, Gasherbrum 1, Broad Peak, and Gasherbrum 2. All of these high peaks in a relatively small area make Gilgit-Baltistan a paradise for mountain climbers, trekkers, photographers, and fishermen.[1]

There are many glaciers in the mountains of Gilgit-Baltistan, with the largest being Baltoro, Batura, Biafo, and Godwin-Austin. A fifth— the largest glacier outside a polar area—is Siachen, which is part of the area disputed by India and Pakistan. India controls Siachen, but armies from both sides regularly skirmish there. More men die from exposure, frostbite, and avalanches than from fighting.[2]

Baltit was the ancient capital of Hunza. The Baltit Fort built high on a ridge served as both a fort for defense and a royal palace. After 750 years the royal residence was moved below the ridge and came to be called Karimabad. Baltit Fort was abandoned and stripped of every-thing of value after 1945. After restoration and rebuilding, Baltit Fort looks like it did in ancient days and is open to the public.

Karimabad has developed a bustling tourist trade. The people are friendly and hospitable. If you happened to be invited to a new friend's home, you might be treated to a meal of *doudo,* which is noodle soup with vegetables, thickened with egg and whole wheat flour. The Hunza people also enjoy apricot soup, which is made with dried apricots, flour, and water.

Farther north on the KKH is Passu, which is the starting point for the famous Two Bridges Walk. The trek itself is easy by trekking standards, but walking over the Hunza River on two rickety-looking suspension bridges is the real adventure. The bridges consist of cables with boards or branches for the footpath. The river looms far below, clearly visible through the gaps in the walkway. Locals can cross the bridges at a run, but trekkers are likely to take it a little slower.

Near the northernmost part of Pakistan is the Khunjerab Pass, which takes a traveler from Pakistan into China. It is possible to travel into China on the KKH with the right papers. Most of the Pakistani

FYI FACT:

The Khyber Railway was completed by the British in 1925. A marvel of engineering, it has 34 tunnels and 92 bridges and cuttings. The gradient is so steep that two engines are required to push and pull a train to its destination.

side of the pass is in the Khunjerab National Park. The pass is one of the only known habitats for the rare curly horned Marco Polo sheep.

If a visitor turns around here and goes back south on the KKH, he or she will go through Gilgit Town. The game of polo reigns here. Polo was once called the game of kings, probably because it was so expensive to play. Polo is a little like playing croquet but on horseback, with two teams swinging at and smacking a wooden ball with long mallets. It's a rough game with many injuries to players and horses. Gilgit has a weeklong polo tournament during the first week of November every year.

The next stop on a tour of Pakistan is Khyber Pakhtunkhwa, which also has a new name.

Two Bridges Walk over the Hunza River

The Khattak sword dance performed by Pashtun tribal members dates back to the fourteenth century. Tribal lore says that the Khattaks danced with swords to warm up before going into battle with their enemies. The dancers perform in a circle and use as many as three swords at once. The drumbeat is fast, as are the steps of the dancers, who display their physical fitness and agility.

Khyber Pakhtunkhwa

The former North-West Frontier Province in Pakistan was renamed Khyber Pakhtunkhwa in April 2010. The change reflected both the importance of the Khyber Pass into Afghanistan and the majority ethnic group or tribe in the province, the Pashtuns.

The ancient Pashtun tribe has many members in Afghanistan. They have been fierce fighters against the United States as it has tried to root out the fundamentalist Islamic Taliban.

To the Pashtuns of Khyber Pakhtunkhwa, their tribes are much more important than their nationalities. Many of the Pakistani Pashtuns sympathize with their Afghan tribal members. This leads to problems, since Pakistan and Afghanistan are supposedly on opposite sides in the War on Terror. There is much skirmishing and fighting in the mountains near the border with Afghanistan.

The biggest cultural influence on Pashtuns is a moral code called *pashtunwali*. Following this code is often more important to Pashtuns than national laws. The key concepts of this code are individual equality, honor, and hospitality. The code insists that Pashtuns must avenge any insults. There is no time limit on avenging the insults, and bloody feuds can last a long time.

Honor for women is the most closely guarded part of the code. Women are very restricted in their contact with men outside the immediate family. Any serious breaking of that part of the code may be punished with death, for either the man or the woman or both.

There are many other native tribes living in the northwestern part of Pakistan. These tribes are mostly located in the Federally Administered Tribal Areas (FATA). The FATA borders Afghanistan and extends midway south in Khyber Pakhtunkhwa into the southern province of Balochistan. The FATA is considered part of Khyber Pakhtunkhwa but is governed by the federal government in Islamabad.[1]

In reality there is little federal control in the FATA. The tribal elders serve as the law. The FATA is off-limits to any travelers. It is a dangerous place, and has become even more so since the beginning of the U.S.-Afghanistan war.

Shalwar kameez

Khyber Pakhtunkhwa's capital city, Peshawar, sits in the middle of the province on the old Grand Trunk Road. This ancient city has often been used as part of a trading route or as a staging point for invasion to the east. It looks up to the west at the Khyber Pass. Refugees from Afghanistan have flooded through the Khyber Pass into Peshawar many times since the 1980s. Thousands of refugees live in camps outside Peshawar.

Peshawar's greatest attraction is the Old City, with its maze of narrow streets leading to bazaars, where shopkeepers and vendors stack their goods high. It's noisy there as rickshaws, horse-drawn carts, and motorcycles make their way through the clogged streets. Afghan merchants are plentiful, as are Afghan and Pashtun men. Women are less visible, but the ones who come to the Old City will likely be dressed in a burka, which is a draped garment that covers a woman from head to toe, or in the traditional *shalwar kameez,* which is a tunic-and-trousers combination.

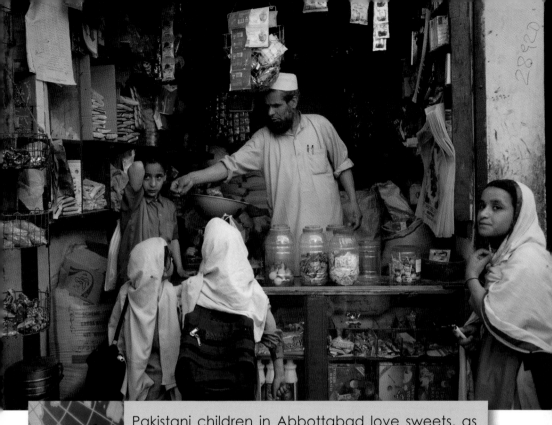

Pakistani children in Abbottabad love sweets, as do many Pakistanis. Schoolgirls stop by the local candy shop for a treat. They may buy some *burfi* or *gulab jamun*. Both popular candies are made of milk and sugar, but *gulab jamun* also has flour. The sweets are soft and velvety.

The city of Abbottabad in Khyber Pakhtunkhwa became famous on May 2, 2011. That day, after many months of training and intelligence gathering, a special U.S. Navy SEAL team landed in a compound in Abbottabad, where they found and killed Osama bin Laden. The al-Qaeda leader was not hiding in a cave in the western mountains of Pakistan. He was living in relative comfort with his family in a large house less than a mile from a Pakistani military academy.

The discovery of Bin Laden brought many new questions about Pakistan's commitment to the War on Terror. Its government denied knowing that he was hiding there. Although many people did not believe that the government was telling the truth, even U.S. Secretary of Defense Robert Gates said there was no solid evidence that Pakistani government leaders knew where Bin Laden was hiding.

Farther north near Chitral on the Afghanistan border are three valleys tucked into the Hindu Kush. The Kalash Valleys—Rumbur, Bumboret, and Birir—have long fascinated outsiders with their unique culture.

The Kalash residents claim to be descendants of Alexander the Great and his army. The great conqueror passed through this area as he made his way to the Indus Valley. He may have camped for a while in the rugged yet beautiful valleys. The Kalash people, alone among ethnic groups in Pakistan, resisted being converted to Islam, Hinduism, or any other regional religions. While the Kalash worship only one god, they pray and offer sacrifices to many spirits, several of which are connected with nature or natural processes. They practice many purification ceremonies to cleanse someone or something that is unclean.

A Kalash girl

For centuries, the Kalash Valley peoples lived an isolated life in their mountain homes until the 1980s, when roads and schools were built in parts of the valleys. With easier access to the valleys, tourists came to see the natural beauty and to witness the people's unique culture. They can pay a fee to enter the valleys. What they see in the villages is different from what is in other Pakistani villages. The women do not wear veils, and visiting Pakistanis often view the Kalash women as not respectable.

The rich fields of the valleys grow wheat, millet, corn, and lentils. Some Kalash herd goats, while others grow mulberries, apricots, apples, and walnuts. There is little meat eaten in the valleys except for the occasional goat.

Wheat has been harvested and stacked in Pakistan, where farmers use a combination of ancient and modern methods.

The Kalash love festivals and celebrate several throughout the year. The festivals involve religious ceremonies, dancing, and feasting. They celebrate Joshi in mid-May in honor of future harvests. The holiday features dancing and family reunions.

The biggest festival is the Chaumos or solstice festival, celebrated for ten days in mid-December. There is much dancing along with religious ceremonies. Foreign tourists who want to participate in the Chaumos must arrive early to be ritually purified. These individuals may need to buy a goat for a sacrifice.

A traveler must go back south a long distance to visit the last province in Pakistan. Balochistan is much different from the lush northern valleys.

Fishing is good on the sea coast of Balochistan, but fishermen are hampered by their poor equipment and methods. The Pakistani government has launched an effort to help these fishermen by providing training and support to allow them to earn a decent living from fishing.

Balochistan

In the southwest corner of Pakistan is the last of the four provinces, Balochistan. This province is the biggest, at 134,050 square miles (347,190 square kilometers), yet has the smallest population—only about 8 million people.

Unlike many parts of Pakistan, Balochistan does not have a monsoon season. It does have the same desert climate, with hot summers and cold winters. In most years moisture is sparse and comes as snow in the winter.

Much of Balochistan is barren, with stony deserts and rocky mountains. The distances between settlements are long and the roads practically nonexistent. There is often unrest among the native Baloch tribes, and the trouble in Afghanistan sometimes spills over the border into Balochistan. Many permits are required before a person can travel anywhere other than the capital of Quetta.

Balochistan is only minimally controlled by the federal or provincial governments. Many tribes live there, including the Baloch, Brahui, and Pashtun, and they take care of their own business. Each tribe has several different branches. About 50 percent of the population lives within 53 miles (85 kilometers) of Quetta.

Quetta has grown up in the midst of relative geographic isolation. Because of political unrest, it has few visitors except those on their way to or from Iran. Quetta has historic ties to Afghanistan and is home to many Afghan refugees. It was rumored that Bin Laden and other al-Qaeda and Taliban officials lived there.

Hanna Lake near Quetta is a popular weekend destination for locals. There are picnic areas, nearby cafés, and a small artificial island in the middle of the lake. Visitors can rent paddleboats to go around the island.

If they were able to visit, tourists would find many attractions, such as bazaars featuring handicrafts. There are Baloch carpets, which are woven with bold geometric designs, and embroidered shirts, caps, and cushion covers that are inlaid with tiny mirrors. The Pashtuns are known worldwide for their intricate embroidered designs on coats and jackets.

The local food specialty is *sajji,* which is a whole roasted leg of lamb lightly seasoned with spices, and eaten with traditional paper-thin bread. The common Afghan dish of *pilau* (rice with meat and raisins) is also popular in Quetta. During the winter, piping hot *murgh* (peppery chicken soup) is available from stalls along the streets.

Quetta residents are huge sports fans. Football (soccer) is the most popular sport there, unlike the rest of Pakistan, where cricket is king. Here, cricket comes in at a close second, then field hockey, boxing,

From left to right, *aloo gobi* (potatoes and cauliflower), *seekh kehbab* (minced meat on skewers), and beef *karahi* (stir-fried steak)

squash, mountain climbing, and caving. The city has produced many winning teams and individuals in these sports.

Bolan Pass is southeast of Quetta and has been a main route for invaders, traders, and nomad caravans as they traveled from Central Asia to India. Now the railroad and the road go through this pass. In the spring, long lines of nomads and camel caravans from Sindh still go through the pass as they bring livestock and goods to sell in the Quetta markets.

Farther southeast is Sibi, another centuries-old town. Near both the Bolan Pass and the Harnai Pass, Sibi has been important to traders. The town is very hot, with temperatures edging toward 120°F (50°C). Sibi is best known for Sibi Mela, a fair held in February. Cattle and horses are the main attraction, and merchants offer tribal handicrafts such as silk, ceramics, and leatherwear.

Not far from Sibi, at the foot of the Bolan Pass, is Mehrgarh, the oldest archaeological site yet discovered on the subcontinent. This farming society appears to be older than the Indus Valley civilization and the civilizations of ancient Egypt and Mesopotamia. Archaeologists believe that the area was inhabited from at least 7000 BCE until around 2000 BCE.[1]

A final stop in Balochistan might be the southern coast on the Arabian Sea. The Makran region borders the Arabian Sea on one side, and has low mountains on the other. It is a desert landscape and has always been thought of as a wild place. Alexander the Great is reported to have marched through this area, losing thousands of men to dehydration and hunger.

The temperatures vary between different parts of the Makran but all are extreme. There are no rivers, so the water supply comes from springs and other underground waterways. However, some land is suitable for growing crops between two of the local mountain chains.

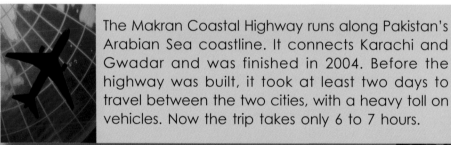

The Makran Coastal Highway runs along Pakistan's Arabian Sea coastline. It connects Karachi and Gwadar and was finished in 2004. Before the highway was built, it took at least two days to travel between the two cities, with a heavy toll on vehicles. Now the trip takes only 6 to 7 hours.

Dates, coconuts, and bananas are grown for export. Grains and pulses are grown for local use.

Visitors are not encouraged to come to the Makran because uprisings in Balochistan are common. The Makran is a hot spot, with frequent bomb and rocket attacks against government-run facilities.

The tour of Pakistan ends where it began—at the Arabian Sea. It would be difficult to visit Pakistan now. It is too dangerous in much of the country. But when peace comes again to the Indus Valley, the Karakoram Mountains, and the Khyber Pass, there will be many wonders to see in this beautiful and mysterious country.

Balochistan urial, a type of wild sheep

Pakistani

Naan

Naan is traditional flat bread that Pakistanis eat with almost any main dish. It is served hot from the oven with such popular dishes as Tandoori chicken and all kinds of kebabs. It is delicious topped with butter or any kind of jelly or jam. It also makes a good crust for pizza toppings.

Ingredients
4 cups all-purpose flour
1 teaspoon baking powder
¼ teaspoon salt
1 egg, beaten
6 tablespoons plain yogurt
3 tablespoons butter
1 cup milk
1 tablespoon poppy seeds, if available

Directions
1. Mix flour, baking powder, and salt together in a large bowl.
2. Stir in egg, yogurt, and 2 tablespoons of the butter.
3. Gradually stir in enough milk to make a soft dough.
4. Cover with a damp cloth and let it sit in a warm place for 2 hours.
5. Preheat oven to 400°F (205°C). Knead dough on a floured surface for 2 or 3 minutes until smooth.
6. Divide dough into 8 pieces. Roll each piece into a ball and then flatten it into ovals about 6 inches long.
7. Brush the underside of each oval with water and place on a greased baking sheet.
8. Brush the top side with the remaining butter and sprinkle it with poppy-seeds if desired.
9. Bake 10 to 15 minutes until the bread is golden brown and a bit puffy.

Pakistani Truck Art

The most popular art in Pakistan can be found rolling down rough Pakistani roads. Heavy duty trucks that haul goods and raw materials across Pakistan sport vivid paintings, wood carvings, metal trim, and other forms of decoration. The paintings on the trucks are often said to have their roots in the decorations that adorned camel caravans centuries ago.

The artisans who decorate the lumbering trucks often gather in neighborhoods to do their work. The Garden Road district in Karachi is a good example. The whole neighborhood is devoted to truck decoration.

Almost any symbol or picture can be found painted on a truck. Truck owners choose the subjects to be painted, and each truck is different. Truck painters are skilled artists, but anyone can create a replica of the famous truck art.

Materials
Colorful cardstock   Scissors
Colored markers   Glue Stick

Instructions
1. A 12 x 12 piece of cardstock makes a good base for your truck art. Cardstock is heavier and has brighter colors than construction paper. Pakistani truck art has bright colors and is crowded with images.
2. You can make the designs with markers or cut out shapes from colored paper and paste them on the base paper. Many Pakistani designs are floral or geometric. You can also make a bright design like the peacock shown. Fill in around the main picture with other smaller designs or cutouts.
3. The cutout method is the easiest. Use scissors to cut out many different shapes of all sizes from colored paper. Arrange these pieces on the base paper in any way that is pleasing to you. Once you like your design, glue the pieces down.

TIMELINE

5000 BCE	Earliest evidence of village life in Pakistan at Mehrgarh.
3300–1800	Indus Valley Civilization thrives.
518	King Darius I of Persia invades.
327–325	Alexander the Great invades Pakistan region but is forced to flee.

CE

c. 711	Muhammad bin Qasin invades Sindh—brings Islam.
c. 870	Shahi dynasty spreads Hinduism.
1526	Babur founds Mughal Empire.
1858	British take over the region, founding the British Raj.
1947	Pakistan is partitioned from India and becomes independent.
1948	Muhammad Ali Jinnah, the founder of Pakistan, dies.
1958	General Ayub Khan takes over in first military coup.
1959	The capital moves from Karachi to Islamabad.
1971	East Pakistan becomes Bangladesh. Zulfikar Ali Bhutto becomes martial law administrator.
1972	Bhutto initiates development of nuclear weapons program.
1977	General Muhammad Zia-ul-Haq takes over in a coup.
1985	Pakistan produces weapons-grade uranium.
1988	General Zia is killed in a plane crash. Benazir Bhutto becomes prime minister.
1990	Nawaz Sharif becomes prime minister.
1994	Benazir Bhutto becomes prime minister again.
1997	Nawaz Sharif becomes prime minister again.
1998	Pakistan conducts its first nuclear tests.
1999	General Musharraf takes over in a coup.
2001	Members of the extremist group al-Qaeda attack the United States on September 11.
2005	A devastating earthquake, with its epicenter near Muzaffarabad, kills 80,000 people.
2007	Benazir Bhutto is assassinated.
2008	Pervez Musharraf resigns, and Asif Ali Zardari becomes president.
2009	Federally Administered Northern Areas are renamed Gilgit-Baltistan.
2010	North-West Frontier Province is renamed Khyber Pakhtunkhwa. After unusually heavy monsoon rains, flooding is widespread.
2011	U.S. Navy SEALS secretly find and kill Osama bin Laden in Abbottabad, Pakistan, where he is believed to have lived in a compound since 2005. Pakistan sees this action as a threat to its sovereignty. U.S.-Pakistan relations continue to fall apart.

Introduction
1. Professor Daniel Waugh and Adela Lee, *Ancient Silk Road Travelers,* "Travelers on the Silk Road," http://www.silk-road.com/artl/srtravelmain.shtml

Chapter 1. The Mighty Indus
1. Sarina Singh, *Pakistan & the Karakoram Highway* (Oakland, California: Lonely Planet Publications, 2008), p. 28.
2. BBC-Religions-Islam: "Mughal Empire (1500s, 1600s)," September 7, 2009. http://www.bbc.co.uk/religion/religions/islam/history/mughalempire_1.shtml

Chapter 2. Pakistan: A Young Country
1. Owen Bennett Jones, *Pakistan; Eye of the Storm* (New Haven and London: Yale University Press, 2009), p. 229.
2. Stanley Wolpert, *Jinnah of Pakistan* (New York: Oxford University Press, 1984), p. 339.

Chapter 3. Generals, Presidents, and Prime Ministers
1. Owen Bennett Jones, *Pakistan; Eye of the Storm* (New Haven and London: Yale University Press, 2009), p. 228.
2. Stephen Cohen, *The Idea of Pakistan* (Washington D.C.: The Brookings Institution, 2004), p. 8.
3. Jones, p. 231–232.
4. Ibid., p. 233.
5. Ibid., p. 20.
6. Ibid., p. 298.

Chapter 4. Sindh Province
1. Alice Albinia, *Empires of the Indus, the Story of a River* (New York: W.W. Norton & Company, Inc., 2008), p. 21.
2. Sarina Singh, *Pakistan & the Karakoram Highway* (Oakland, California: Lonely Planet Publications, 2008), p. 179.

Chapter 5. The Punjab
1. Alice Albinia, *Empires of the Indus, the Story of a River* (New York: W.W. Norton & Company, Inc., 2008), p. 253.

Chapter 6. Islamabad and Rawalpindi
1. Wildlife of Pakistan: "Margalla Hills National Park," http://www.wildlifeofpakistan.com/ProtectedAreasofPakistan/Margalla_NP.htm

Chapter 7. Azad Jammu & Kashmir
1. Dr. A. Naeem, Dr. Qaisar Ali, Muhammad Javed, Zakir Hussain, Syed Muhammad Ali, Irshad Ahmed, and Muhammad Ashraf, "Pakistan: A Summary Report on Muzaffarabad Earthquake," *ReliefWeb,* November 7, 2005, http://reliefweb.int/node/414607
2. Fareed Zarkaria, "Urgent Cry for Help as Death Toll Rises from Pakistan Flooding," August 16, 2010, http://news.blogs.cnn.com/2010/08/16/urgent-cry-for-help-as-death-toll-rises-from-pakistan-flooding/?iref=storysearch
3. *Fox News:* "Pakistan Flood Victims Going into Debt to Rebuild," October 17, 2010, http://www.foxnews.com/world/2010/10/17/pakistan-flood-victims-going-debt-rebuild/

Chapter 8. Gilgit-Baltistan
1. Gilgit-Baltistan Tourism Department: "Adventure Tourism," http://www.visitgilgitbaltistan.gov.pk/adventure.html
2. Dr. Nayyar Hashmey, *Wonders of Pakistan,* "Glaciers of Pakistan," http://wondersofpakistan.wordpress.com/category/glaciers-of-pakistan/

Chapter 9. Khyber Pakhtunkhwa
1. Federally Administered Tribal Areas (FATA): "Administrative System," http://fata.gov.pk/index.php?option=com_content&view=article&id=50&Itemid=84

Chapter 10. Balochistan
1. Sarina Singh, *Pakistan & the Karakoram Highway* (Oakland, California: Lonely Planet Publications, 2008), p. 153.
2. *BBC News:* "Stone Age Man Used Dentist Drill," April 6, 2006, http://news.bbc.co.uk/2/hi/science/nature/4882968.stm

FURTHER READING

Books

Abbott, David. *Pakistan*. London: Franklin Watts, 2010.

Price, Sean Stewart. *Benazir Bhutto*. Mankato, Minnesota: Heinemann-Raintree, 2009.

Qamar, Amjed. *Beneath My Mother's Feet*. New York: Atheneum, 2008.

Thomson, Sarah, Greg Mortenson, and David Oliver. *Three Cups of Tea: One Man's Journey to Change the World . . . One Child at a Time*. London: Puffin, 2009.

Works Consulted

Albinia, Alice. *Empires of the Indus, the Story of a River*. New York: W.W. Norton & Company, Inc., 2008.

BBC-Religions-Islam: "Mughal Empire (1500s, 1600s)," September 7, 2009. http://www.bbc.co.uk/religion/religions/islam/history/mughalempire_1.shtml

Bhutto, Benazir. *Reconciliation; Islam, Democracy, and the West*. New York: HarperCollins Publishers, 2008.

Cohen, Stephen Philip. *The Idea of Pakistan*. Washington, D.C.: Brookings Institution Press, 2004.

Federally Administered Tribal Areas (FATA): "Administrative System." http://fata.gov.pk/index.php?option=com_content&view=article&id=50&Itemid=84

Fox News: "Pakistan Flood Victims Going into Debt to Rebuild." October 17, 2010. http://www.foxnews.com/world/2010/10/17/pakistan-flood-victims-going-debt-rebuild/

Gilgit-Baltistan Tourism Department: "Adventure Tourism." http://www.visitgilgitbaltistan.gov.pk/adventure.html

Hashmey, Dr. Nayyar. *Wonders of Pakistan,* "Glaciers of Pakistan." http://wondersofpakistan.wordpress.com/category/glaciers-of-pakistan/

Jones, Owen Bennett. *Pakistan: Eye of the Storm*. New Haven and London: Yale University Press, 2009.

Levy, Adrian, and Catherine Scott-Clark. *Deception: Pakistan, the United States, and the Secret Trade in Nuclear Weapons*. New York: Walker & Company, 2007.

Mittmann, Karin, and Zafar Ihsan. *Culture Shock! Pakistan*. Portland, Oregon: Graphic Arts Center Publishing Company, 2000.

Musharraf, Pervez. *In the Line of Fire: A Memoir*. New York: Simon & Schuster, Inc., 2006.

Naeem, Dr. A., Dr. Qaisar Ali, Muhammad Javed, Zakir Hussain, Syed Muhammad Ali, Irshad Ahmed, and Muhammad Ashraf. "Pakistan: A Summary Report on Muzaffarabad Earthquake." *ReliefWeb,* November 7, 2005. http://reliefweb.int/node/414607

Perlez, Jane. "Pakistani Sentenced to Death May Get a Pardon." *The New York Times,* November 22, 2010. http://www.nytimes.com/2010/11/23/world/asia/23pstan.html?_r=1&ref=pakistan

Singh, Sarina, Lindsay Brown, Paul Clammer, Rodney Cocks, John Mock, and Kimberley O'Neil. *Pakistan & the Karakoram Highway.* Oakland, California: Lonely Planet Publications, 2008.

Sinkler, Adrian, editor. *The World's Hot Spots: Pakistan.* Farmington Hills, Michigan: Greenhaven Press, 2003.

Waugh, Prof. Daniel, and Adela Lee. *Ancient Silk Road Travelers,* "Travelers on the Silk Road." http://www.silk-road.com/artl/srtravelmain.shtml

Wildlife of Pakistan: "Margalla Hills National Park." http://www.wildlifeofpakistan.com/ProtectedAreasofPakistan/Margalla_NP.htm

Wolpert, Stanley. *Jinnah of Pakistan.* New York: Oxford University Press, 1984.

Zarkaria, Fareed. "Urgent Cry for Help as Death Toll Rises from Pakistan Flooding." *CNN,* August 16, 2010. http://news.blogs.cnn.com/2010/08/16/urgent-cry-for-help-as-death-toll-rises-from-pakistan-flooding/?iref=storysearch

On the Internet

Balochistan: Gateway to All Government Services of Balochistan
http://www.balochistan.gov.pk/

CIA—*The World Factbook*
https://www.cia.gov/library/publications/the-world-factbook/geos/pk.html

How Stuff Works: "The Indus River"
http://geography.howstuffworks.com/asia/the-indus-river.htm

Kids Around the World—Learn More About Pakistan
http://www.katw.org/pages/sitepage.cfm?id=119

Kids Konnect—Pakistan
http://www.kidskonnect.com/subject-index/26-countriesplaces/327-pakistan.html

Ministry of Information and Broadcasting: Government of Pakistan
http://www.infopak.gov.pk/default.aspx

Pakistan Herald: "Details of Muhammad Ali Jinnah"
http://pakistanherald.com/Profile/Muhammad-Ali-Jinnah-1173

Wildlife of Pakistan
http://wildlifeofpakistan.com/

autonomy (aw-TAH-nuh-mee)—The power or right to govern oneself.

cease-fire (SEES-fyr)—The stopping of weapons use during a war, often temporary.

cholera (KAH-luh-ruh)—An often deadly infection spread by contaminated water.

corruption (kuh-RUP-shun)—Loss of honesty or integrity; dishonest behavior such as bribery.

coup (KOO)—Short for *coup d'etat,* the sudden overthrow of a legitimate government by another group, usually the military.

glacier (GLAY-shur)—A large mass of ice formed in cold regions from compacted snow, often slowly moving downhill.

maharajah (mah-hah-RAH-jah)—A Hindu prince.

monsoon (mon-SOON)—A wind system in the Indian Ocean that changes direction seasonally and causes heavy rains; it can also refer to a rainy season.

municipal (myoo-NIH-sih-pul)—Having to do with a local government or unit of government.

nomad (NOH-mad)—A member of a tribe or group that has no fixed home and moves from place to place.

partition (par-TIH-shen)—To divide into parts or sections.

plateau (plaa-TOH)—A high, level area of land.

refugee (REH-fyoo-jee)—A person who leaves his or her home country in order to find safety from war or persecution.

solstice (SOHL-stis)—Either of two times in the year, in June and December, when the sun is farthest from the equator.

sovereignty (SAH-vrin-tee)—Supreme power; freedom from outside control.

uranium (yur-AY-nee-um)—A metal element that breaks down easily; when it does, its nuclear energy is used to produce electricity and weapons.

urial (OOR-ee-ul)—A wild mountain sheep of Asia that is reddish brown.

Bonnie Hinman is the author of more than 25 books for young people, including one about Peru and another about Panama. This is the first time she has written about a Middle Eastern country. However, Hinman has been interested in the Indus Valley Civilization since elementary school. She has always been fascinated by the Cradle of Civilization in the Middle East. Hinman graduated from Missouri State University and lives in Southwest Missouri with her husband, Bill, near her children and five grandchildren.